A Snowflake Fell

Poems About Winter

Cold and raw the north wind doth blow,
Bleak in the morning early;
All the hills are covered with snow,
And winter's now come fairly.

Traditional

To Jeffrey, Christopher, Wade and Hannah,
who love the snow — L. W.

For Yuiko, Gakkuto and Kazuo, with love — H. H.

Barefoot Books
124 Walcot Street
Bath, BA1 5BG

This book was typeset in Post Antiqua Bold, DellaRobbia and Garamond
The illustrations were prepared in pastel and watercolour

Graphic design by Barefoot Books, Bath
Colour separation by Grafiscan, Verona
Printed and bound in Singapore by Tien Wah Press (Pte) Ltd

This book has been printed on 100% acid-free paper

ISBN 1-84148-050-9

British Cataloguing-in-Publication Data: a catalogue record
for this book is available from the British Library

1 3 5 7 9 8 6 4 2

A Snowflake Fell

Poems About Winter

compiled by **Laura Whipple**

illustrated by **Hatsuki Hori**

Barefoot Books
Celebrating Art and Story

Contents

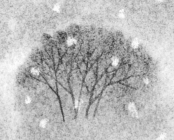

Introduction

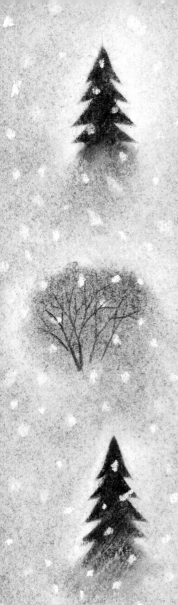

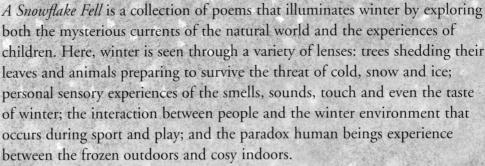

A Snowflake Fell is a collection of poems that illuminates winter by exploring
both the mysterious currents of the natural world and the experiences of
children. Here, winter is seen through a variety of lenses: trees shedding their
leaves and animals preparing to survive the threat of cold, snow and ice;
personal sensory experiences of the smells, sounds, touch and even the taste
of winter; the interaction between people and the winter environment that
occurs during sport and play; and the paradox human beings experience
between the frozen outdoors and cosy indoors.

Many of the poems focus on what happens to the earth and its creatures
when winter arrives. In 'Old Man Winter', the poet Nancy Wood uses ideas
from the Native American Taos people in portraying winter as an old man who
arrives to grip the world in a tight embrace of rest. Several poems describe
animals that scurry to store food, compete for seeds, grow thick coats and
migrate. Even in the bleakest winter setting, the pulse of nature beats in the
shining aurora borealis and in animals hibernating beneath the snow.

In contrast, many of the poems feature more personal experiences of winter.
Children often remember winter as what they do and much of this activity
is associated with joy and excitement. Sledging, ice skating, playing hockey,
skiing, piling on winter clothes, making snowmen, riding in a sleigh and
catching snowflakes on their tongues are all heightened experiences that many
children have during the winter months. A child may also feel the dreamlike
quality that winter can evoke, described by Michael Spooner in his poem
'Winter Nights' — lying down on a bed of snow, looking into the icy, starry
sky and feeling a sense of awe. Similarly, Christine Boyka Kluge's 'New Year

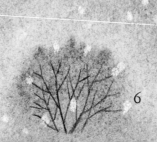

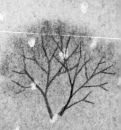

Snowbird' offers the wondrous vision of a child swinging through night-time snow to let the stars tickle her nose. There is also a warmer, more comfortable experience which is associated with wintertime, the feeling of being indoors and away from winter's icy chill. What could be cosier than sitting with your stuffed animals and your feet in fuzzy slippers by the warm furnace as described by Gary Soto, or smelling the friendly scent of popcorn in 'Let's Pop The Corn' by Constance Levy?

But winter can also be seen as a time of danger, of biting cold, and hard, sharp ice. James Whitcomb Riley stirs up chilling images in his poem 'Winter Fancies', with the winter wind that snows and snarls and raves and shrieks. Cheeks become chapped, noses turn red and ears tingle in Laura Richards' 'A Sleigh-ride', and winter ponds wear 'skins of bright hardened ice' in Jane Yolen's 'Winter Song of the Weasel'.

Not only will children respond to the content of these poems, but they will also delight in the sounds of the words. If read aloud, the onomatopoeic sound of the mouse's tiny feet flicking across the ground can be heard in Marilyn Singer's 'Deer Mouse', the repetition of the letter 's' in 'Winter Song of the Weasel' is not only alliterative, but echoes the hissing sound of falling snow. The word 'cold' in 'Cold Morning' by Felice Holman brings a chill by its repetition. For an older child, the beautiful word choices of Ted Hughes in 'Goose' create visual pictures — 'smoking mouth', 'iceberg breath', 'flame of evening', and a 'rumpus of walrus'.

So, pop some corn; put your fuzzy slippers on, and use your imagination to experience the sharp smell of winter air, the sound of ice skates on a frozen pond, the touch of snow on your face and even the taste of the first snowflake as it falls from the sky.

Laura Whipple

Jack Frost

The door was shut, as doors should be,
   Before you went to bed last night;
Yet Jack Frost has got in, you see,
   And left your window silver white.

He must have waited till you slept;
   And not a single word he spoke,
But pencilled o'er the panes and crept
   Away again before you woke.

And now you cannot see the hills
   Nor fields that stretch beyond the lane;
But there are fairer things than these
   His fingers traced on every pane.

Rocks and castles towering high;
   Hills and dales, and streams and fields;
And knights in armour riding by,
   With nodding plumes and shining shields.

And butterflies with gauzy wings;
   And herds of cows and flocks of sheep;
And fruit and flowers and all the things
   You see when you are sound asleep.

He paints them on the windowpane
   In fairy lines with frozen steam;
And when you wake you see again
   The lovely things you saw in dream.

Gabriel Setoun

from **Winter Song of the Weasel**

…Winter fields wear smocks of snow
disguising all who sleep below
in caves and warrens, dens and lairs,
the wintering of chucks and bears
whose dreams are fat and dark and deep.
They make their living out of sleep.
Winter ponds wear skins of bright
hardened ice that show not light.
I see no fish beneath that sheen.
What was once cannot be seen
in winter.

And so I change.
I reproduce upon my hide
the wintering I feel inside.

Jane Yolen

Deer Mouse

get   get get get   get
   get
      out of the nest
   get
      into the cold
get   get get get
   get
      food
      lots of food
   get
      seeds
      berries
      nuts
      bugs
      bark
get enough to last
get enough to store
get more
get   get get get   get
   get going
      move
        hustle
don't rustle
don't squeak
    beware
    danger in the air
get busy
get done
get   get get get
   get out of here
      run

Marilyn Singer

The Snow

The snow, in bitter cold,
Fell all the night;
And we awoke to see
The garden white.

Beyond the gate, soft feet
In silence go,
Beyond the frosted pane
White shines the snow.

F. Ann Elliott

Cold Morning

My breath
makes a cloud of steam
float before my
cold face,
float upon the cold air.
My lips cold,
my breath hot
blows out
white clouds.
Look
what I have done!
Made a warm cloud
in the cold air
of the world.

Felice Holman

Old Man Winter

Old Man Winter blew in on a cloud from the north
And lay down on the mountaintops
Covering them with snow.
His fingers reached down to the valleys below
Stealing the leaves from the trees.
His hands closed around the water
Gripping it with ice.
His breath roared out from his lips
Stopping all the streams at their source.
The feet of Old Man Winter walked upon the earth
Freezing all the grass.
When he was through
Old Man Winter curled up and went to sleep
Drawing into himself
All beasts
All land
All men.

Nancy Wood

Snowman

One day we built a snowman
  We made him out of snow.
You'd ought to see how fine he was
  All white from top to toe.
We poured some water on him
  And froze him — legs and ears,
And when we went indoors to bed,
  I said he'd last two years.
But in the night, a warmer kind
  Of wind began to blow
And Winter cried and ran away,
  And with it ran the snow.
And in the morning when we went,
  To bid our friend, 'Good day',
There wasn't any snowman there,
  He'd melted all away.

Anonymous

16

Winter Poem

once a snowflake fell
on my brow and i loved
it so much and i kissed
it and it was happy and called its cousins
and brothers and a web
of snow engulfed me then
i reached to love them all
and i squeezed them and they became
a spring rain and i stood perfectly
still and was a flower

Nikki Giovanni

Joe

We feed the birds in winter,
And outside in the snow
We have a tray of many seeds
For many birds of many breeds
And one grey squirrel named Joe.
    But Joe comes early,
    Joe comes late,
    And all the birds
    Must stand and wait.
And waiting there for Joe to go
Is pretty cold work in the snow.

David McCord

The Winter Tree

The winter tree
Is fast asleep.
She dreams, in reams
Of snow knee-deep,
Of children climbing
Up her trunk,
Of white-tailed deer
And grey chipmunk,
Of picnics,
Hammocks,
And short sleeves,
And leaves
  And leaves
    And leaves
      and leaves.

Douglas Florian

My Mother's Got Me Bundled Up

My mother's got me bundled up
in tons of winter clothes,
you could not recognise me
if I did not have a nose.
I'd wear much less, but she'd get mad
if I dared disobey her,
so I stay wrapped from head to toe
in layer after layer.

I am wearing extra sweaters,
I am wearing extra socks,
my galoshes are so heavy
that my ankles seem like rocks.
I am wearing scarves and earmuffs,
I am wearing itchy pants,
my legs feel like they're swarming
with a million tiny ants.

My mittens are enormous
and my coat weighs more than me,
my woollen hat and ski mask
make it difficult to see.
It's hard to move, and when I try
I waddle, then I flop,
I'm the living, breathing model
of a walking clothing shop.

Jack Prelutsky

New Year Snowbird

In the night, in the snow, on the swings,
my glistening boots become wings
I fly through the shadows waiting to pounce
on the porch light
where tiny snowflakes bounce
like confetti

Are you ready?
My whistling wings pull me up and up
The snow becomes faraway stars on my toes
When I jump towards the light
I close my eyes tight and
let the stars tickle my nose

Christine Boyka Kluge

22

Ice Skates

Two ball-point pens are what I have,
and one slick sheet of paper.
Now. Ready? Begin:
Roll some scrolls,
swing some rings,
twirl some curls,
loop some hoops,
whirl some swirls,
mark some arcs,
toe some bows,
reel some wheels,
twine some vines.
All done:
the largest,
the greatest,
the coolest
scribble-scrabble
ever.

Sylvia Cassedy

Ice Hockey

Swish, slash,
  my skates
    crash on ice

quick stick
cuts to puck

    guide it
slide it
    swerve it
curve it

see a hole —
  WHACK!

GOAL!

Laura Whipple

25

from **Furnace**

…Once, when I was really little,
Snow layered our front lawn
With hard, hard white.
The house was cold, quiet.
I jumped from bed,
Turned on the heater,
And jumped back in bed
With my stuffed dolphin,
My bear, my cat with its tail gone,
The animals of sleep
And cuddle. I whispered
My leftover dreams,
And when I was ready,
I gathered my animals
Into my arms,
Carried them to the furnace,
And we sat in its glow….

We raised our paws, fins,
And hands to the gust
Of furnace heat.
Even my slippers,
Twin rabbits on my feet,
Shivered to get warm.
What was happiness
More than me laughing
And my toes
Wiggling the noses
Of my rabbits?

Gary Soto

from **The Night Rainbow**

…Above our heads
shimmering curtains
move and part.
The drapery gathers and
falls.
Over the forests of Musquakie land,
the light begins to flare and twist.
Shining spirits
shake their streaming hair.
We whistle them down the sky.
The dancers bend and leap and run.
Their cloaks unfold and fold
in ruby light.
In dazzling moccasins
they whirl up
and down the dark slopes of air.
The pale fringes of their shawls
hang in ruby light
against the stars.

Barbara Juster Esbensen

A Sleigh-ride

Ting! ring! The sleigh bells jingle
   Merrily over the frozen snow,
Cheeks a-glow and ears a-tingle,
   Tumble in children, here we go!

Ting! ring! The sleigh-bells jingle!
   Get along, Dobbin! Go along, Jack!
Bells and voices merrily mingle,
   Swift we fly as an arrow's track.

Ting! ring! The sleigh-bells jingle!
   Nose cold, Tommy? Here rub it with snow!
Toes ache, Ned? Just kick till they tingle,
   Thump! thump! thump! on the dasher, so!

Ting! ring! The sleigh-bells jingle!
   Snow-wreaths fly like snow-sea's foam.
Sweet bells, sweet laugh, hark! how they mingle!
   Tumble out, children, here we're at home!

Laura E. Richards

30

The Snowman

Out in the garden
The snowman stands
With his black button eyes
And twigs for hands,

With his old torn hat
And his floor-mop hair.
He hasn't even
A coat to wear.

He likes the winter
And the sparrows that come
To perch on his shoulder
When their toes are numb.

The wind blows north
And the wind blows south,
But he stands and grins
With a pipe in his mouth.

Whichever way
The wind may blow,
He does not mind
The frost and snow.

But when daffodils flutter
On a fine spring day
He'll dribble and squelch
And melt away,

And the sparrows will find
Next day at dawn
A little grey heap
On the garden lawn.

James K. Baxter

Goose

The White Bear, with smoking mouth, embraces
All the North.
The Wild Goose listens.

South, south —
                                    the Goose stretches his neck
Over the glacier.

And high, high
Turns the globe in his hands.

Hunts with his pack from star to star.
Sees the sun far down behind the world.

Sinks through fingers of light, with apricot breast,
To startle sleeping farms, at apple dawn,
With iceberg breath. …

Homesick
Smells the first flower of the Northern Lights —

Clears the Lamb's cry, wrestles heaven,
Sets the globe turning.

Clears the dawns — a compass tolling,
North, north.

North, north.

Wingbeat wading the flame of evening.

Till he dips his eyes
In the whale's music

Among the boom
of calving glaciers

And wooing of wolves
And rumpus of walrus.

Ted Hughes

Downhill

This time let me steer
and you be in back.
Do my feet go here?
Do I follow this track?
No no, I'm really okay,
I know what I'm doing.
Hang on tight….Hey!
We're going, we're going.
Everything's white.
Everything's slick.
Lean to the right —
I mean to the left. Quick.
Look out, look out. Jump!

This is the lousiest sled I've ever seen.
Next time you be in front
and I'll lean.

Richard J. Margolis

Skiing

Skiing is like being
part of a mountain.
On the early morning run
before the crowds begin,
my skis make
    little blizzards
as they plough
    through untouched powder
to leave fresh tracks
    in the blue-white snow.
My body bends and turns
    to catch each
bend and turn
    the mountain takes;
and I am the mountain
and the mountain is me.

Bobbi Katz

35

Winter Fancies

Winter without
     And warmth within;
The winds may shout
     And the storm begin;
The snows may pack
     At the window-pane,
And the skies grow black,
     And the sun remain
Hidden away
     The livelong day —
But here — in here is the warmth of May!

…Then blow, winds, blow!
     And rave and shriek,
And snarl and snow,
     Till your breath grows weak —
While here in my room
     I'm as snugly shut
As a glad little worm
     In the heart of a nut!

James Whitcomb Riley

Let's Pop The Corn

Let's pop the corn
and fire the logs
and take off our shoes
and wiggle our toes
and sit on the rug
and talk.
Let's eat all the popcorn
and pop some more,
and do again
what we did before.

They fit:
the popcorn, the fire
the pops and crackles
the flickers and crunches
the wiggles
the warmth
the winter weather
and nice
soft
talking
together.

Constance Levy

Winter Nights

I want to lie down
      where the snow
  is deep.
Lie on my back
    where the silence of snow
   is thick,
and where great
     white drifts
    drop into curves
      and hollows
round the bases of trees.

I want to look up
     straight up
  from a bed
in deep snow
    and see the stars
      wheeling round
   as if I lay silently
     over the pin
  that keeps them
stuck to earth.

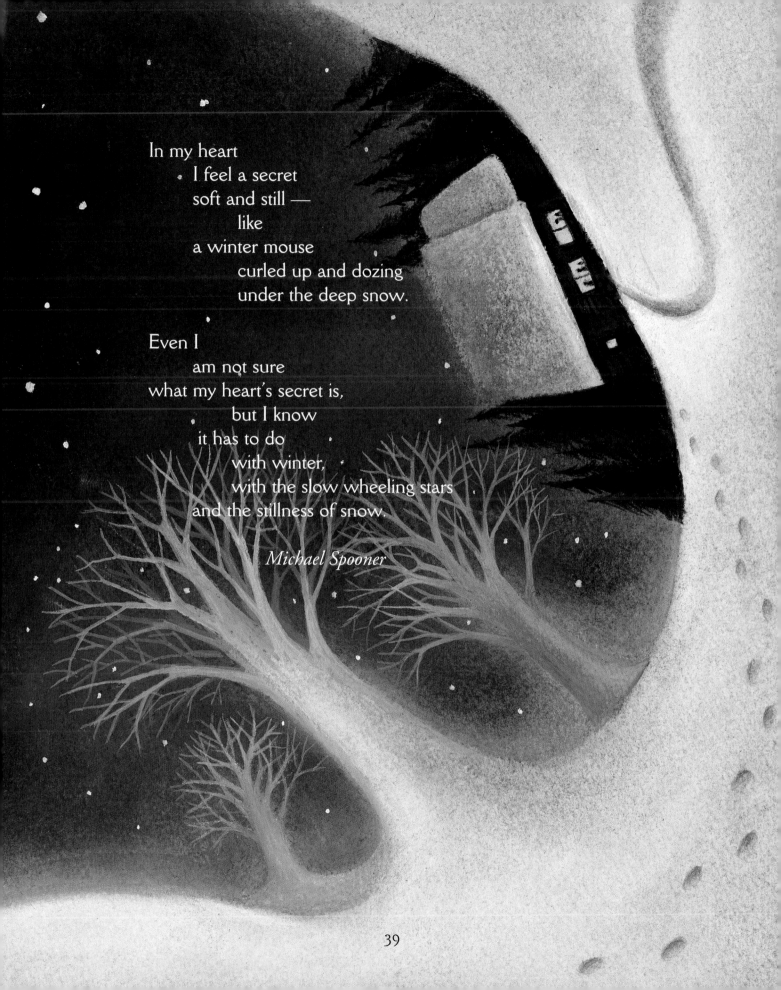

In my heart
      I feel a secret
      soft and still —
            like
a winter mouse
      curled up and dozing
      under the deep snow.

Even I
      am not sure
what my heart's secret is,
      but I know
      it has to do
      with winter,
      with the slow wheeling stars
and the stillness of snow.

Michael Spooner

Acknowledgements

'Jack Frost' by Gabriel Setoun from *A Child's World*, published by The Bodley Head, 1896. Excerpts from 'Winter Song of the Weasel' by Jane Yolen, copyright © Jane Yolen from *Ring of Earth: A Child's Book of Seasons*, published by Harcourt, Inc., 1986. 'Deer Mouse' by Marilyn Singer, copyright © by Marilyn Singer, from *Turtle in July*, published by Macmillan Publishing Company, 1989. 'The Snow' by F. Ann Elliott from *The Book of 1000 Poems*, published by HarperCollins *Publishers* Ltd, 1994. 'Cold Morning' by Felice Holman, copyright © Felice Holman from *I Hear You Smiling and Other Poems*, published by Charles Scribner's Sons, 1989. 'Old Man Winter' copyright © by Nancy Wood, from *Many Winters*, published by Doubleday and Co. Inc., 1974. All rights reserved. 'Winter Poem' by Nikki Giovanni, copyright © Nikki Giovanni, from *The Sun is So Quiet: Poems*, published by Henry Holt and Company, Inc., 1996. 'Joe' from *One at a Time* by David McCord. Copyright © 1952 by David McCord. By permission of Little, Brown and Company, (Inc). 'The Winter Tree' copyright © 1999 by Douglas Florian, used by permission of HarperCollins *Publishers* Ltd. 'My Mother's Got Me Bundled Up' copyright © 1984 by Jack Prelutsky, used by permission of HarperCollins *Publishers* Ltd. 'New Year Snowbird' copyright © 1998 by Christine Boyka Kluge from *Cricket Magazine*, January 1998 Vol. 25, number 5. 'Ice Skates' by Sylvia Cassedy, from *Zoomrimes: Poems About Things That Go*, HarperCollins *Publishers* Ltd, 1993. Copyright © 1993 by the Estate of Sylvia Cassedy. Reprinted by permission of Ellen Cassedy. 'Ice Hockey' copyright © Laura Whipple, 2003. Excerpts from 'Furnace' in *Canto Familiar*, copyright © 1995 by Gary Soto, reprinted by permission of Harcourt, Inc. 'The Night Rainbow' by Barbara Juster Esbensen. Copyright © 2000 by Tory Esbense. Reprinted by permission of Orchard Books, an imprint of Scholastic, Inc. 'A Sleigh-ride' by Laura E. Richards, copyright © 1932 by Laura E. Richards from *The Golden Flute: An Anthology of Poetry for Young Children*, published by the Jon Day Company. 'The Snowman' copyright © by James K. Baxter from *The Tree House and Other Poems for Children*, published by Price Milburn, 1974. 'Goose' by Ted Hughes, copyright © 1981 by Ted Hughes, from *Under the North Star*, used by permission of Faber & Faber Ltd. 'Downhill' by Richard J. Margolis, reprinted with the permission of Simon & Schuster Books for Young Readers, an imprint of Simon & Schuster Children's Publishing Division from *Secrets of a Small Brother* by Richard J. Margolis. Text copyright © 1984 by Richard J. Margolis. 'Skiing', copyright © 1971 by Bobbi Katz. Used with permission of the author. 'Winter Fancies' by James Whitcomb Riley from *Rhymes of Childhood*, published by The Bobbs-Merill Company Publishers, 1898. 'Let's Pop the Corn' copyright © by Constance Levy. Used by permission of Marian Reiner for the author. 'Winter Nights' from *A Moon in Your Lunchbox, Poems by Michael Spooner* copyright © 1993 by Michael Spooner. Reprinted by permission of Henry Holt and Company, LLC.

The publishers have made every effort to contact holders of copyright material. If you have not received our correspondence, please contact us for inclusion in future editions.

Barefoot Books
Celebrating Art and Story

At Barefoot Books, we celebrate art and story with books that open the hearts and minds of children from all walks of life, inspiring them to read deeper, search further, and explore their own creative gifts. Taking our inspiration from many different cultures, we focus on themes that encourage independence of spirit, enthusiasm for learning, and acceptance of other traditions. Thoughtfully prepared by writers, artists and storytellers from all over the world, our products combine the best of the present with the best of the past to educate our children as the caretakers of tomorrow.

www.barefootbooks.com